# 50 Big Flavor Ingredients

By: Kelly Johnson

# Table of Contents

- Garlic Butter Shrimp
- Chipotle Chicken Tacos
- Lemon Caper Chicken Piccata
- Balsamic Glazed Brussels Sprouts
- Thai Basil Beef
- Honey Sriracha Glazed Salmon
- Roasted Garlic Mashed Potatoes
- Moroccan-Spiced Carrots
- Miso Glazed Eggplant
- Spicy Gochujang Noodles
- Chili Crisp Fried Rice
- Smoked Paprika Roast Chicken
- Anchovy Garlic Pasta
- Harissa Lamb Meatballs
- Za'atar Roasted Cauliflower
- Kimchi Grilled Cheese
- Bourbon Glazed Pork Chops

- Chimichurri Steak
- Tandoori Chicken Legs
- Green Curry Coconut Soup
- Firecracker Shrimp
- Mango Habanero Wings
- Truffle Oil Mac and Cheese
- Cajun Blackened Fish
- Thai Peanut Noodles
- Roasted Red Pepper Hummus
- Spicy Sichuan Tofu Stir-Fry
- Jalapeño Cheddar Cornbread
- Maple Dijon Roasted Vegetables
- Buffalo Cauliflower Bites
- Black Garlic Ramen
- Banh Mi Sliders
- Pesto Zucchini Noodles
- Gremolata Roasted Lamb
- Sweet Chili Chicken Stir-Fry
- Spanish Paprika Potatoes

- Lemon Dill Baked Cod
- Toasted Sesame Bok Choy
- Cumin-Spiced Sweet Potato Tacos
- Soy Maple Glazed Tempeh
- Saffron Tomato Risotto
- Garlic Confit Pasta
- Mole Chicken Enchiladas
- Wasabi Pea Crusted Tuna
- Roasted Fig and Goat Cheese Flatbread
- Orange Glazed Duck Breast
- Coconut Lemongrass Chicken
- Jalapeño Pineapple Fried Rice
- Chorizo Stuffed Peppers
- Five Spice Crispy Tofu

**Garlic Butter Shrimp**

**Ingredients:**

- 1 lb large shrimp, peeled and deveined
- 4 tbsp unsalted butter
- 4 cloves garlic, minced
- Juice of 1 lemon
- 2 tbsp chopped parsley
- Salt and pepper, to taste

**Instructions:**

1. Melt butter in a skillet over medium heat. Add garlic and sauté until fragrant.
2. Add shrimp, season with salt and pepper, and cook 2–3 minutes per side.
3. Squeeze lemon juice over shrimp and sprinkle with parsley.
4. Serve hot with pasta, rice, or crusty bread.

**Chipotle Chicken Tacos**

**Ingredients:**

- 1 lb chicken thighs, boneless and skinless
- 2 chipotle peppers in adobo, chopped
- 1 tbsp adobo sauce
- 2 garlic cloves, minced
- 1 tbsp lime juice
- 1 tbsp olive oil
- Salt, to taste
- Corn tortillas and toppings (lettuce, salsa, avocado, etc.)

**Instructions:**

1. Marinate chicken with chipotle, garlic, lime juice, oil, and salt for 30 minutes.
2. Grill or pan-sear until cooked through and slightly charred.
3. Slice and serve in tortillas with desired toppings.

**Lemon Caper Chicken Piccata**

**Ingredients:**

- 2 chicken breasts, butterflied and pounded thin
- 1/2 cup flour
- 2 tbsp olive oil
- 1/2 cup chicken broth
- 1/4 cup lemon juice
- 2 tbsp capers
- 2 tbsp butter
- Salt and pepper

**Instructions:**

1. Dredge chicken in flour, season with salt and pepper.
2. Sear in oil over medium heat until golden and cooked through.
3. Remove chicken; add broth, lemon juice, and capers to pan.
4. Simmer, then stir in butter. Return chicken and coat with sauce.

**Balsamic Glazed Brussels Sprouts**

**Ingredients:**

- 1 lb Brussels sprouts, halved
- 2 tbsp olive oil
- Salt and pepper
- 2 tbsp balsamic vinegar
- 1 tbsp honey

**Instructions:**

1. Toss Brussels sprouts with oil, salt, and pepper. Roast at 400°F for 25 minutes.
2. Mix balsamic vinegar and honey in a pan; reduce slightly.
3. Drizzle glaze over roasted sprouts and toss to coat.

**Thai Basil Beef (Pad Kra Pao)**

**Ingredients:**

- 1 lb ground beef
- 4 garlic cloves, minced
- 2 Thai chilies (or 1 jalapeño), minced
- 2 tbsp soy sauce
- 1 tbsp oyster sauce
- 1 tbsp fish sauce
- 1 tsp sugar
- 1 cup Thai basil leaves
- Cooked jasmine rice
- Fried egg (optional)

**Instructions:**

1. Sauté garlic and chili in oil. Add beef and cook until browned.
2. Add sauces and sugar; stir well.
3. Toss in basil leaves just before serving.
4. Serve with rice and fried egg if desired.

**Honey Sriracha Glazed Salmon**

**Ingredients:**

- 4 salmon fillets
- 2 tbsp honey
- 1 tbsp sriracha
- 1 tbsp soy sauce
- 1 tbsp lime juice
- 1 garlic clove, minced

**Instructions:**

1. Mix glaze ingredients.
2. Brush over salmon and bake at 400°F for 12–15 minutes or until cooked through.
3. Broil for 2 minutes to caramelize glaze if desired.

## Roasted Garlic Mashed Potatoes

**Ingredients:**

- 2 lbs Yukon gold potatoes, peeled and chopped
- 1 head garlic
- 1/2 cup butter
- 1/2 cup heavy cream
- Salt and pepper

**Instructions:**

1. Roast garlic at 400°F wrapped in foil with a drizzle of oil, for 35–40 minutes.
2. Boil potatoes until tender, then drain.
3. Mash with butter, cream, and squeezed roasted garlic.
4. Season to taste.

**Moroccan-Spiced Carrots**

**Ingredients:**

- 1 lb carrots, sliced
- 2 tbsp olive oil
- 1 tsp cumin
- 1/2 tsp cinnamon
- 1/2 tsp paprika
- Salt and pepper
- 1 tbsp lemon juice
- Fresh parsley, chopped

**Instructions:**

1. Toss carrots with oil and spices.
2. Roast at 400°F for 25–30 minutes.
3. Drizzle with lemon juice and sprinkle with parsley before serving.

**Miso Glazed Eggplant**

**Ingredients:**

- 2 medium eggplants, sliced into 1-inch thick rounds
- 3 tbsp miso paste
- 1 tbsp soy sauce
- 1 tbsp rice vinegar
- 1 tbsp honey
- 2 tbsp sesame oil
- 2 tbsp chopped green onions
- 1 tbsp sesame seeds

**Instructions:**

1. Preheat oven to 400°F (200°C).
2. Arrange eggplant slices on a baking sheet.
3. Mix miso paste, soy sauce, rice vinegar, honey, and sesame oil in a bowl.
4. Brush the miso mixture generously on each eggplant slice.
5. Roast for 25 minutes until tender and caramelized.
6. Sprinkle with green onions and sesame seeds before serving.

**Spicy Gochujang Noodles**

**Ingredients:**

- 8 oz noodles (soba, udon, or spaghetti)
- 2 tbsp gochujang (Korean chili paste)
- 1 tbsp soy sauce
- 1 tbsp sesame oil
- 1 tbsp rice vinegar
- 2 tsp sugar
- 1 garlic clove, minced
- 1/2 cup sliced cucumber (optional)
- 1 tbsp sesame seeds
- Green onions for garnish

**Instructions:**

1. Cook noodles according to package instructions. Drain and set aside.
2. In a bowl, mix gochujang, soy sauce, sesame oil, rice vinegar, sugar, and garlic.
3. Toss cooked noodles with the gochujang sauce until well coated.
4. Garnish with cucumber, sesame seeds, and green onions. Serve hot or cold.

**Chili Crisp Fried Rice**

**Ingredients:**

- 3 cups cooked rice (preferably day-old)
- 2 tbsp chili crisp oil
- 2 eggs, scrambled
- 1 cup mixed vegetables (carrot, peas, corn)
- 2 tbsp soy sauce
- 1 tbsp sesame oil
- 2 garlic cloves, minced
- 2 green onions, chopped
- Salt and pepper to taste

**Instructions:**

1. Heat sesame oil in a large skillet or wok. Add garlic and cook until fragrant.
2. Add mixed vegetables and cook until tender.
3. Push the veggies to one side and scramble the eggs on the other side of the skillet.
4. Add cooked rice, soy sauce, and chili crisp oil. Stir-fry for a few minutes until well combined.
5. Season with salt, pepper, and garnish with green onions before serving.

**Smoked Paprika Roast Chicken**

**Ingredients:**

- 1 whole chicken (3-4 lbs)
- 2 tbsp olive oil
- 2 tsp smoked paprika
- 1 tsp garlic powder
- 1 tsp onion powder
- 1 tsp dried thyme
- Salt and pepper to taste
- 1 lemon, halved
- 4 sprigs fresh rosemary

**Instructions:**

1. Preheat oven to 425°F (220°C).
2. Pat chicken dry and rub with olive oil. Season with smoked paprika, garlic powder, onion powder, thyme, salt, and pepper.
3. Stuff the chicken with lemon halves and rosemary.
4. Roast in the oven for 1 hour and 15 minutes, or until the internal temperature reaches 165°F (75°C).
5. Let rest for 10 minutes before carving.

## Anchovy Garlic Pasta

**Ingredients:**

- 8 oz pasta (spaghetti or linguine)
- 4 tbsp olive oil
- 6 anchovy fillets, chopped
- 4 garlic cloves, minced
- 1/4 tsp red pepper flakes
- 1/4 cup chopped parsley
- Freshly grated Parmesan (optional)

**Instructions:**

1. Cook pasta according to package instructions.
2. Heat olive oil in a large skillet over medium heat. Add anchovies, garlic, and red pepper flakes.
3. Cook for 2–3 minutes until anchovies melt and garlic is fragrant.
4. Toss the cooked pasta in the skillet with the anchovy mixture.
5. Garnish with parsley and Parmesan before serving.

# Harissa Lamb Meatballs

**Ingredients:**

- 1 lb ground lamb
- 1/4 cup breadcrumbs
- 2 tbsp harissa paste
- 1 egg
- 2 garlic cloves, minced
- 1 tsp cumin
- 1 tsp coriander
- Salt and pepper to taste
- 2 tbsp olive oil
- Fresh cilantro for garnish

**Instructions:**

1. Preheat oven to 375°F (190°C).
2. In a bowl, mix ground lamb, breadcrumbs, harissa, egg, garlic, cumin, coriander, salt, and pepper.
3. Form mixture into 1-inch meatballs and place on a baking sheet.
4. Heat olive oil in a pan and sear meatballs for 2 minutes on each side.
5. Transfer to the oven and bake for 15 minutes until cooked through.
6. Garnish with cilantro before serving.

## Za'atar Roasted Cauliflower

**Ingredients:**

- 1 medium cauliflower, cut into florets
- 3 tbsp olive oil
- 2 tbsp za'atar seasoning
- Salt and pepper to taste
- Fresh parsley for garnish

**Instructions:**

1. Preheat oven to 400°F (200°C).
2. Toss cauliflower florets with olive oil, za'atar, salt, and pepper.
3. Spread on a baking sheet and roast for 25–30 minutes, turning halfway through.
4. Garnish with fresh parsley before serving.

**Kimchi Grilled Cheese**

**Ingredients:**

- 2 slices bread (sourdough or your choice)
- 2 tbsp butter
- 2 slices cheddar cheese
- 1/4 cup kimchi, chopped
- 1 tbsp mayonnaise (optional)

**Instructions:**

1. Butter one side of each slice of bread.
2. Place one slice of cheese, a spoonful of kimchi, and another slice of cheese on one slice of bread.
3. Top with the other slice of bread, buttered side up.
4. Grill in a pan over medium heat until golden brown and cheese is melted, about 3–4 minutes per side.

**Bourbon Glazed Pork Chops**

**Ingredients:**

- 4 boneless pork chops
- 1/4 cup bourbon
- 1/4 cup brown sugar
- 1/4 cup soy sauce
- 2 tbsp Dijon mustard
- 2 tbsp apple cider vinegar
- 1 tbsp olive oil
- Salt and pepper to taste

**Instructions:**

1. Season pork chops with salt and pepper.
2. In a small saucepan, combine bourbon, brown sugar, soy sauce, mustard, and vinegar. Simmer for 5–7 minutes until thickened.
3. Heat olive oil in a pan over medium-high heat and sear pork chops for 4–5 minutes per side.
4. Brush the bourbon glaze over the chops and cook for an additional 2 minutes.
5. Serve with extra glaze on the side.

**Chimichurri Steak**

**Ingredients:**

- 2 boneless ribeye or flank steaks
- 1/4 cup fresh parsley, finely chopped
- 3 tbsp fresh oregano, finely chopped
- 4 garlic cloves, minced
- 1/4 cup red wine vinegar
- 1/2 cup olive oil
- 1 tsp red pepper flakes
- Salt and pepper to taste

**Instructions:**

1. Preheat grill or skillet over medium-high heat.
2. Season steaks with salt and pepper on both sides.
3. Grill steaks for 4-5 minutes per side for medium-rare, or to your preferred doneness.
4. In a small bowl, mix together parsley, oregano, garlic, vinegar, olive oil, red pepper flakes, salt, and pepper to make the chimichurri sauce.
5. Let the steaks rest for 5 minutes, then drizzle with chimichurri sauce before serving.

## Tandoori Chicken Legs

**Ingredients:**

- 8 chicken drumsticks
- 1/2 cup plain yogurt
- 2 tbsp tandoori masala
- 1 tbsp ground cumin
- 1 tbsp ground coriander
- 1 tsp turmeric
- 1 tsp garam masala
- 1 tbsp lemon juice
- 2 cloves garlic, minced
- 1-inch ginger, minced
- Salt to taste

**Instructions:**

1. In a bowl, combine yogurt, tandoori masala, cumin, coriander, turmeric, garam masala, lemon juice, garlic, ginger, and salt to make the marinade.
2. Coat the chicken legs in the marinade and refrigerate for at least 2 hours (or overnight for best results).
3. Preheat oven to 400°F (200°C).
4. Arrange chicken on a baking sheet lined with parchment paper and bake for 30-35 minutes, until the chicken is cooked through and the skin is crispy.

5. Serve hot with naan or rice.

**Green Curry Coconut Soup**

**Ingredients:**

- 1 tbsp coconut oil
- 1 tbsp green curry paste
- 1 can (14 oz) coconut milk
- 2 cups vegetable or chicken broth
- 1 cup sliced mushrooms
- 1 cup baby spinach
- 1/2 cup chopped carrots
- 1/2 cup chopped bell pepper
- 1 tbsp fish sauce
- 1 tbsp brown sugar
- 1 lime (juiced)
- Fresh cilantro for garnish

**Instructions:**

1. Heat coconut oil in a large pot over medium heat. Add green curry paste and cook for 2-3 minutes until fragrant.
2. Add coconut milk and broth to the pot and stir well.
3. Add mushrooms, spinach, carrots, and bell pepper. Bring to a simmer and cook for 10-12 minutes until vegetables are tender.

4. Stir in fish sauce, brown sugar, and lime juice. Taste and adjust seasoning as needed.

5. Serve hot, garnished with fresh cilantro.

## Firecracker Shrimp

**Ingredients:**

- 1 lb shrimp, peeled and deveined
- 1/2 cup all-purpose flour
- 1/2 cup cornstarch
- 1/2 tsp salt
- 1/2 tsp pepper
- 1/2 cup buttermilk
- 1/4 cup hot sauce (such as sriracha)
- 1 tbsp honey
- 1/4 cup mayonnaise
- Vegetable oil for frying

**Instructions:**

1. In a bowl, combine flour, cornstarch, salt, and pepper.
2. Dip shrimp into buttermilk, then coat in the flour mixture.
3. Heat oil in a large skillet over medium-high heat. Fry shrimp in batches until golden and crispy, about 2-3 minutes per side.
4. In a separate bowl, mix hot sauce, honey, and mayonnaise to make the firecracker sauce.
5. Toss fried shrimp in the sauce until coated, then serve hot.

**Mango Habanero Wings**

**Ingredients:**

- 10-12 chicken wings
- 1 ripe mango, peeled and chopped
- 1 habanero pepper, seeds removed and chopped
- 1/4 cup honey
- 2 tbsp lime juice
- 1 tbsp olive oil
- Salt and pepper to taste

**Instructions:**

1. Preheat oven to 400°F (200°C).
2. Arrange wings on a baking sheet and season with salt and pepper. Bake for 25-30 minutes, flipping halfway through, until crispy and golden.
3. In a blender, combine mango, habanero, honey, lime juice, and olive oil. Blend until smooth.
4. Toss the cooked wings in the mango habanero sauce and serve hot.

## Truffle Oil Mac and Cheese

**Ingredients:**

- 8 oz elbow macaroni
- 2 tbsp butter
- 2 tbsp all-purpose flour
- 2 cups whole milk
- 2 cups shredded cheddar cheese
- 1/2 cup grated Parmesan cheese
- 1-2 tbsp truffle oil
- Salt and pepper to taste
- Fresh parsley for garnish (optional)

**Instructions:**

1. Cook macaroni according to package instructions, drain and set aside.
2. In a saucepan, melt butter over medium heat. Stir in flour and cook for 1-2 minutes.
3. Gradually add milk, whisking constantly until the sauce thickens.
4. Stir in cheddar cheese and Parmesan until melted and smooth.
5. Add truffle oil, salt, and pepper, then stir in cooked macaroni.
6. Serve hot, garnished with fresh parsley if desired.

**Cajun Blackened Fish**

**Ingredients:**

- 4 white fish fillets (such as tilapia, catfish, or snapper)
- 2 tbsp Cajun seasoning
- 1 tbsp paprika
- 1 tbsp garlic powder
- 1/2 tsp cayenne pepper
- 1 tbsp olive oil
- 1 tbsp butter
- Lemon wedges for serving

**Instructions:**

1. Preheat a cast-iron skillet over high heat.
2. Mix Cajun seasoning, paprika, garlic powder, and cayenne pepper in a small bowl.
3. Coat fish fillets in the seasoning mixture on both sides.
4. Add olive oil and butter to the skillet. Once melted, add the fish fillets and cook for 3-4 minutes per side, until blackened and cooked through.
5. Serve with lemon wedges.

**Thai Peanut Noodles**

**Ingredients:**

- 8 oz rice noodles
- 1/4 cup peanut butter
- 2 tbsp soy sauce
- 1 tbsp honey
- 2 tbsp lime juice
- 1 garlic clove, minced
- 1 tbsp sesame oil
- 1/4 tsp red pepper flakes
- Chopped peanuts and cilantro for garnish

**Instructions:**

1. Cook rice noodles according to package instructions, drain and set aside.
2. In a bowl, whisk together peanut butter, soy sauce, honey, lime juice, garlic, sesame oil, and red pepper flakes to make the sauce.
3. Toss cooked noodles in the peanut sauce until well coated.
4. Garnish with chopped peanuts and cilantro before serving.

**Roasted Red Pepper Hummus**

**Ingredients:**

- 1 can (15 oz) chickpeas, drained and rinsed
- 2 roasted red peppers (jarred or homemade)
- 2 tbsp tahini
- 2 tbsp olive oil
- 1 garlic clove, minced
- 1 tbsp lemon juice
- 1/2 tsp cumin
- Salt and pepper to taste
- Water as needed for consistency

**Instructions:**

1. In a food processor, combine chickpeas, roasted red peppers, tahini, olive oil, garlic, lemon juice, cumin, salt, and pepper.
2. Blend until smooth. Add water a little at a time to reach desired consistency.
3. Taste and adjust seasoning as needed.
4. Serve with pita, crackers, or fresh vegetables.

**Spicy Sichuan Tofu Stir-Fry**

**Ingredients:**

- 1 block firm tofu, drained and cubed
- 2 tbsp vegetable oil
- 1 red bell pepper, sliced
- 1 yellow onion, sliced
- 2 garlic cloves, minced
- 1 tbsp fresh ginger, minced
- 2 tbsp soy sauce
- 1 tbsp rice vinegar
- 1 tbsp Sichuan peppercorns
- 2 tbsp chili paste (or 1 tbsp chili flakes)
- 1 tbsp sesame oil
- Green onions for garnish

**Instructions:**

1. Heat vegetable oil in a large pan or wok over medium-high heat. Add tofu cubes and cook until crispy on all sides, about 5-7 minutes. Remove tofu and set aside.

2. In the same pan, add bell pepper, onion, garlic, and ginger. Stir-fry for 3-4 minutes until softened.

3. Add soy sauce, rice vinegar, Sichuan peppercorns, and chili paste. Stir to combine.

4. Return tofu to the pan and toss everything together in the sauce. Drizzle with sesame oil and garnish with green onions.

5. Serve with steamed rice.

**Jalapeño Cheddar Cornbread**

**Ingredients:**

- 1 cup cornmeal
- 1 cup all-purpose flour
- 1/4 cup sugar
- 1 tbsp baking powder
- 1/2 tsp salt
- 1 cup milk
- 2 eggs
- 1/2 cup unsalted butter, melted
- 1 cup shredded sharp cheddar cheese
- 2-3 jalapeños, finely chopped (seeds removed for less heat)

**Instructions:**

1. Preheat oven to 375°F (190°C). Grease a 9x9-inch baking dish or cast-iron skillet.
2. In a large bowl, mix cornmeal, flour, sugar, baking powder, and salt.
3. In another bowl, whisk together milk, eggs, and melted butter.
4. Pour the wet ingredients into the dry ingredients and stir until combined.
5. Fold in the shredded cheddar cheese and chopped jalapeños.
6. Pour the batter into the prepared dish and bake for 25-30 minutes, until golden brown and a toothpick inserted comes out clean.

7. Serve warm.

## Maple Dijon Roasted Vegetables

**Ingredients:**

- 2 cups carrots, peeled and chopped
- 2 cups Brussels sprouts, halved
- 1 large sweet potato, peeled and cubed
- 2 tbsp olive oil
- 2 tbsp maple syrup
- 1 tbsp Dijon mustard
- 1 tsp garlic powder
- Salt and pepper to taste

**Instructions:**

1. Preheat oven to 400°F (200°C).
2. In a large bowl, toss the carrots, Brussels sprouts, and sweet potato with olive oil, maple syrup, Dijon mustard, garlic powder, salt, and pepper.
3. Spread the vegetables out on a baking sheet in a single layer.
4. Roast for 25-30 minutes, stirring halfway through, until vegetables are tender and lightly caramelized.
5. Serve hot.

## Buffalo Cauliflower Bites

**Ingredients:**

- 1 head cauliflower, cut into florets
- 1 cup all-purpose flour
- 1 cup water
- 1 tsp garlic powder
- 1 tsp paprika
- Salt and pepper to taste
- 1/2 cup buffalo sauce
- 2 tbsp melted butter
- Ranch dressing for serving

**Instructions:**

1. Preheat oven to 425°F (220°C).
2. In a bowl, whisk together flour, water, garlic powder, paprika, salt, and pepper until smooth.
3. Dip cauliflower florets into the batter and place them on a greased baking sheet.
4. Bake for 20-25 minutes until golden and crispy.
5. In a separate bowl, mix buffalo sauce and melted butter.
6. Toss baked cauliflower in the buffalo sauce mixture until well coated.
7. Serve with ranch dressing on the side.

## Black Garlic Ramen

**Ingredients:**

- 4 oz ramen noodles
- 1 tbsp vegetable oil
- 2 garlic cloves, minced
- 1 tbsp black garlic paste
- 2 cups chicken or vegetable broth
- 1 tbsp soy sauce
- 1 tsp sesame oil
- 1/2 tsp chili oil (optional)
- Soft-boiled egg, for garnish
- Green onions, for garnish
- Toasted sesame seeds, for garnish

**Instructions:**

1. Cook ramen noodles according to package instructions, then drain and set aside.
2. In a pot, heat vegetable oil over medium heat. Add minced garlic and black garlic paste. Sauté for 1-2 minutes until fragrant.
3. Add broth, soy sauce, sesame oil, and chili oil (if using). Bring to a simmer and cook for 5 minutes.
4. Add the cooked ramen noodles to the pot and stir to combine.

5. Serve topped with a soft-boiled egg, green onions, and toasted sesame seeds.

**Banh Mi Sliders**

**Ingredients:**

- 12 slider buns
- 1 lb ground pork
- 2 tbsp soy sauce
- 1 tbsp hoisin sauce
- 1 tbsp fish sauce
- 2 garlic cloves, minced
- 1 tbsp fresh ginger, minced
- 1/4 cup mayonnaise
- 2 tbsp sriracha sauce
- 1/2 cucumber, thinly sliced
- 1 small carrot, julienned
- Fresh cilantro leaves

**Instructions:**

1. In a bowl, combine ground pork, soy sauce, hoisin sauce, fish sauce, garlic, and ginger. Form into 12 small patties.
2. Heat a skillet over medium heat and cook the patties for 4-5 minutes per side, until fully cooked.
3. Mix mayonnaise and sriracha sauce together in a bowl.

4. To assemble, spread sriracha mayo on the bottom half of each slider bun. Add a pork patty, followed by cucumber slices, carrot julienne, and cilantro leaves.

5. Top with the other half of the slider bun and serve.

## Pesto Zucchini Noodles

**Ingredients:**

- 4 medium zucchinis, spiralized into noodles
- 1/4 cup pesto sauce (store-bought or homemade)
- 1 tbsp olive oil
- 1 tbsp pine nuts (optional)
- Grated Parmesan cheese for garnish

**Instructions:**

1. Heat olive oil in a large pan over medium heat. Add zucchini noodles and sauté for 3-4 minutes until tender but still firm.
2. Remove from heat and toss with pesto sauce.
3. Garnish with pine nuts and grated Parmesan cheese before serving.

**Gremolata Roasted Lamb**

**Ingredients:**

- 1 rack of lamb (about 1-1.5 lbs)
- 2 tbsp olive oil
- Salt and pepper to taste
- 1/4 cup fresh parsley, finely chopped
- 2 garlic cloves, minced
- Zest of 1 lemon

**Instructions:**

1. Preheat oven to 400°F (200°C).
2. Season the rack of lamb with olive oil, salt, and pepper.
3. Roast the lamb for 25-30 minutes for medium-rare (or adjust to your preferred doneness).
4. While the lamb roasts, mix parsley, garlic, and lemon zest to make the gremolata.
5. After the lamb is roasted, rest for 10 minutes.
6. Serve the lamb topped with the gremolata.

**Sweet Chili Chicken Stir-Fry**

**Ingredients:**

- 2 boneless, skinless chicken breasts, sliced into thin strips
- 1 tbsp vegetable oil
- 1 bell pepper, sliced
- 1 carrot, julienned
- 1 zucchini, sliced
- 2 garlic cloves, minced
- 1/4 cup sweet chili sauce
- 2 tbsp soy sauce
- 1 tbsp rice vinegar
- 1 tsp sesame oil
- 1/2 tsp ginger, minced
- Green onions for garnish
- Sesame seeds for garnish

**Instructions:**

1. Heat vegetable oil in a large pan or wok over medium-high heat. Add chicken and cook until browned and cooked through, about 5-7 minutes.

2. Remove chicken from the pan and set aside. In the same pan, add bell pepper, carrot, zucchini, garlic, and ginger. Stir-fry for 3-4 minutes.

3. In a small bowl, whisk together sweet chili sauce, soy sauce, rice vinegar, and sesame oil.

4. Return the chicken to the pan and pour the sauce over the mixture. Toss everything to coat and cook for another 2-3 minutes.

5. Garnish with green onions and sesame seeds. Serve with steamed rice.

**Spanish Paprika Potatoes**

**Ingredients:**

- 4 medium potatoes, peeled and cut into cubes
- 2 tbsp olive oil
- 1 tsp smoked paprika
- 1/2 tsp garlic powder
- 1/2 tsp onion powder
- Salt and pepper to taste
- Fresh parsley for garnish

**Instructions:**

1. Preheat the oven to 400°F (200°C).
2. Toss the potato cubes with olive oil, smoked paprika, garlic powder, onion powder, salt, and pepper.
3. Spread the potatoes in a single layer on a baking sheet.
4. Roast for 25-30 minutes, flipping halfway through, until crispy and golden.
5. Garnish with fresh parsley and serve.

**Lemon Dill Baked Cod**

**Ingredients:**

- 4 cod fillets
- 1 lemon, sliced
- 2 tbsp olive oil
- 2 tbsp fresh dill, chopped
- Salt and pepper to taste
- 1 tbsp fresh parsley, chopped (optional)

**Instructions:**

1. Preheat the oven to 375°F (190°C).
2. Place the cod fillets on a baking sheet lined with parchment paper. Drizzle with olive oil and season with salt and pepper.
3. Top each fillet with lemon slices and chopped dill.
4. Bake for 15-20 minutes or until the fish flakes easily with a fork.
5. Garnish with fresh parsley and serve with steamed vegetables or rice.

## Toasted Sesame Bok Choy

**Ingredients:**

- 4 baby bok choy, halved
- 1 tbsp sesame oil
- 1 tbsp soy sauce
- 1 tsp honey
- 1 tsp toasted sesame seeds
- 1 garlic clove, minced
- 1 tsp ginger, minced
- Green onions for garnish

**Instructions:**

1. Heat sesame oil in a large skillet or wok over medium heat.
2. Add bok choy, cut side down, and cook for 3-4 minutes until slightly browned.
3. Add garlic and ginger to the pan and cook for another 1-2 minutes.
4. Drizzle with soy sauce and honey, stirring to combine.
5. Sprinkle with toasted sesame seeds and garnish with green onions.
6. Serve as a side dish with rice or noodles.

**Cumin-Spiced Sweet Potato Tacos**

**Ingredients:**

- 2 medium sweet potatoes, peeled and diced
- 1 tbsp olive oil
- 1 tsp cumin
- 1/2 tsp smoked paprika
- Salt and pepper to taste
- 8 small corn tortillas
- 1/2 cup crumbled feta or cotija cheese
- 1/4 cup fresh cilantro, chopped
- Lime wedges for serving

**Instructions:**

1. Preheat the oven to 400°F (200°C).
2. Toss sweet potato cubes with olive oil, cumin, smoked paprika, salt, and pepper.
3. Spread the sweet potatoes on a baking sheet and roast for 20-25 minutes, flipping halfway through, until tender.
4. Warm the tortillas in a skillet over low heat.
5. To assemble the tacos, spoon roasted sweet potatoes onto each tortilla. Top with crumbled cheese, cilantro, and a squeeze of lime.
6. Serve immediately.

**Soy Maple Glazed Tempeh**

**Ingredients:**

- 1 package tempeh, sliced into 1/2-inch strips
- 2 tbsp soy sauce
- 2 tbsp maple syrup
- 1 tbsp rice vinegar
- 1 tsp sesame oil
- 1 garlic clove, minced
- 1 tsp fresh ginger, minced
- 1 tbsp sesame seeds for garnish
- Green onions for garnish

**Instructions:**

1. In a small bowl, whisk together soy sauce, maple syrup, rice vinegar, sesame oil, garlic, and ginger.
2. Heat a nonstick skillet over medium heat and add tempeh slices. Cook for 3-4 minutes per side until golden.
3. Pour the soy maple glaze over the tempeh and cook for another 2-3 minutes until the sauce thickens.
4. Garnish with sesame seeds and green onions.
5. Serve with rice or steamed vegetables.

**Saffron Tomato Risotto**

**Ingredients:**

- 1 tbsp olive oil
- 1 small onion, finely chopped
- 2 garlic cloves, minced
- 1 cup Arborio rice
- 1/4 tsp saffron threads
- 1/2 cup white wine (optional)
- 3 cups vegetable broth, heated
- 1 can (14.5 oz) diced tomatoes, drained
- 1/2 cup grated Parmesan cheese
- Salt and pepper to taste
- Fresh basil for garnish

**Instructions:**

1. In a small bowl, steep saffron threads in 1/4 cup warm water for 10 minutes.
2. Heat olive oil in a large skillet over medium heat. Add onion and garlic and sauté for 3-4 minutes.
3. Stir in Arborio rice and cook for 1-2 minutes until lightly toasted.
4. Pour in white wine (if using) and cook until absorbed.

5. Add heated vegetable broth, one ladle at a time, stirring continuously until the liquid is absorbed before adding more.

6. After 10 minutes, stir in saffron water and tomatoes. Continue adding broth and stirring for about 20 minutes until the rice is creamy and tender.

7. Remove from heat and stir in Parmesan cheese.

8. Season with salt and pepper, and garnish with fresh basil.

9. Serve hot.

**Garlic Confit Pasta**

**Ingredients:**

- 1 lb pasta (spaghetti or linguine works well)
- 1 cup olive oil
- 10 garlic cloves, peeled
- 1 tsp fresh thyme (optional)
- 1/2 tsp red pepper flakes (optional)
- Fresh parsley for garnish
- Grated Parmesan cheese for serving

**Instructions:**

1. In a small saucepan, combine olive oil, garlic cloves, thyme, and red pepper flakes. Heat over low heat for about 30-40 minutes, until the garlic becomes soft and golden (do not let it brown).
2. Meanwhile, cook pasta according to package instructions. Reserve 1/2 cup of pasta water and drain the rest.
3. Remove the garlic from the oil and mash it with a fork.
4. Toss the cooked pasta with the garlic oil, adding reserved pasta water as needed for consistency.
5. Garnish with fresh parsley and grated Parmesan cheese.
6. Serve warm.

## Mole Chicken Enchiladas

**Ingredients:**

- 2 cups cooked shredded chicken
- 8 corn tortillas
- 1 cup mole sauce (store-bought or homemade)
- 1/2 cup shredded cheese (cheddar or Mexican blend)
- 1/4 cup sour cream
- 1/4 cup chopped cilantro
- 1 small onion, finely chopped
- 1 tbsp vegetable oil
- Salt and pepper to taste

**Instructions:**

1. Preheat the oven to 350°F (175°C).
2. Heat the vegetable oil in a skillet over medium heat. Sauté the chopped onion until softened, about 5 minutes.
3. Add the shredded chicken to the skillet and toss to combine with the onions. Season with salt and pepper.
4. Warm the tortillas in a skillet or microwave.
5. Pour 1/2 cup of mole sauce into the bottom of a baking dish.
6. Fill each tortilla with the chicken mixture and roll it up. Place each rolled tortilla seam-side down in the baking dish.

7. Pour the remaining mole sauce over the enchiladas and sprinkle with shredded cheese.

8. Cover with foil and bake for 20 minutes.

9. Remove the foil and bake for an additional 5 minutes, or until the cheese is melted and bubbly.

10. Garnish with sour cream and chopped cilantro. Serve hot.

## Wasabi Pea Crusted Tuna

**Ingredients:**

- 4 tuna steaks (6 oz each)
- 1 cup wasabi peas, crushed
- 2 tbsp soy sauce
- 1 tbsp sesame oil
- 1 tsp fresh ginger, minced
- 1 tbsp rice vinegar
- Salt and pepper to taste
- 1 tbsp sesame seeds (optional)
- 1 green onion, chopped for garnish

**Instructions:**

1. In a bowl, combine soy sauce, sesame oil, rice vinegar, and minced ginger. Season with salt and pepper.
2. Place the tuna steaks in the marinade and let them sit for at least 10 minutes.
3. Crush the wasabi peas into small pieces using a food processor or by placing them in a plastic bag and pounding with a rolling pin.
4. Press each tuna steak into the crushed wasabi peas, ensuring it is evenly coated on both sides.
5. Heat a skillet or grill pan over medium-high heat. Cook the tuna steaks for 2-3 minutes per side for rare, or longer for your desired doneness.

6. Garnish with sesame seeds and chopped green onions. Serve immediately.

## Roasted Fig and Goat Cheese Flatbread

**Ingredients:**

- 1 package flatbread (or pizza dough)
- 8 fresh figs, sliced
- 4 oz goat cheese, crumbled
- 1 tbsp olive oil
- 1 tbsp honey
- 1 tsp balsamic vinegar
- Fresh thyme leaves
- Salt and pepper to taste

**Instructions:**

1. Preheat the oven to 400°F (200°C).
2. Place the flatbread on a baking sheet and brush with olive oil.
3. Arrange the sliced figs evenly over the flatbread.
4. Crumble the goat cheese over the figs.
5. Drizzle with honey and balsamic vinegar, then sprinkle with fresh thyme.
6. Season with salt and pepper.
7. Roast in the oven for 12-15 minutes, or until the edges are crispy and the cheese is slightly melted.
8. Serve warm as an appetizer or main dish.

**Orange Glazed Duck Breast**

**Ingredients:**

- 4 duck breasts
- 1/2 cup fresh orange juice
- 2 tbsp soy sauce
- 1 tbsp honey
- 1 tbsp rice vinegar
- 1 tbsp olive oil
- 1 garlic clove, minced
- Salt and pepper to taste
- Orange zest for garnish

**Instructions:**

1. Score the skin of the duck breasts with a sharp knife.

2. Heat olive oil in a skillet over medium-high heat. Season the duck breasts with salt and pepper.

3. Place the duck breasts skin-side down in the skillet and cook for 6-8 minutes, until the skin is crispy.

4. Flip the duck breasts and cook for another 4-5 minutes for medium-rare, or longer for desired doneness.

5. While the duck is cooking, combine orange juice, soy sauce, honey, rice vinegar, and garlic in a small saucepan. Bring to a simmer and cook for 5-7 minutes until thickened.

6. Remove the duck from the skillet and let it rest.

7. Pour the orange glaze over the duck breasts and garnish with orange zest.

8. Serve immediately with vegetables or mashed potatoes.

**Coconut Lemongrass Chicken**

**Ingredients:**

- 4 chicken breasts or thighs
- 1 can (14 oz) coconut milk
- 2 stalks lemongrass, chopped
- 1 lime, juiced
- 2 garlic cloves, minced
- 1 tsp ginger, minced
- 1 tbsp soy sauce
- 1 tbsp brown sugar
- Fresh cilantro for garnish
- Salt and pepper to taste

**Instructions:**

1. In a blender or food processor, combine coconut milk, lemongrass, lime juice, garlic, ginger, soy sauce, and brown sugar. Blend until smooth.
2. Pour the mixture into a shallow dish and add the chicken breasts or thighs. Marinate for at least 30 minutes or overnight in the refrigerator.
3. Preheat the grill or skillet over medium heat.
4. Cook the chicken for 6-7 minutes per side, or until fully cooked through.
5. Garnish with fresh cilantro before serving.

6. Serve with rice or vegetables.

**Jalapeño Pineapple Fried Rice**

**Ingredients:**

- 2 cups cooked rice (preferably cold)
- 1 tbsp vegetable oil
- 1 small onion, diced
- 2 garlic cloves, minced
- 1 jalapeño, diced (seeds removed for less heat)
- 1/2 cup pineapple, chopped
- 2 eggs, scrambled
- 2 tbsp soy sauce
- 1 tsp sesame oil
- 1/4 cup green onions, chopped
- Salt and pepper to taste

**Instructions:**

1. Heat vegetable oil in a large skillet or wok over medium-high heat. Add the onion and garlic and sauté for 2-3 minutes until softened.

2. Add the jalapeño and pineapple to the pan and cook for another 2-3 minutes.

3. Push the vegetables to the side of the pan and scramble the eggs on the other side. Once scrambled, mix them into the vegetables.

4. Add the cold rice to the pan and stir to combine.

5. Drizzle with soy sauce and sesame oil, stirring to evenly coat.

6. Season with salt and pepper.

7. Garnish with chopped green onions and serve hot.

**Chorizo Stuffed Peppers**

**Ingredients:**

- 4 bell peppers, tops cut off and seeds removed
- 1 lb chorizo sausage
- 1/2 cup cooked rice
- 1/4 cup shredded cheese (Mexican blend or cheddar)
- 1/4 cup onion, chopped
- 2 garlic cloves, minced
- 1/2 cup diced tomatoes
- 1 tsp cumin
- Salt and pepper to taste

**Instructions:**

1. Preheat the oven to 375°F (190°C).
2. In a skillet, cook the chorizo over medium heat until browned and cooked through.
3. Add the onion and garlic and sauté for 3-4 minutes until softened.
4. Stir in the rice, diced tomatoes, cumin, salt, and pepper.
5. Stuff the bell peppers with the chorizo mixture and place them in a baking dish.
6. Sprinkle the cheese on top of each stuffed pepper.
7. Cover with foil and bake for 25-30 minutes.

8. Remove the foil and bake for another 5-10 minutes, until the cheese is melted and bubbly.

9. Serve hot.

**Five Spice Crispy Tofu**

**Ingredients:**

- 1 block firm tofu, drained and cubed
- 1 tbsp cornstarch
- 1 tbsp five-spice powder
- 1 tbsp soy sauce
- 1 tbsp sesame oil
- 1/2 tsp garlic powder
- 1/4 tsp salt
- 1 tbsp vegetable oil for frying
- Green onions for garnish

**Instructions:**

1. Press the tofu to remove excess moisture, then cut it into cubes.
2. In a bowl, mix cornstarch, five-spice powder, soy sauce, sesame oil, garlic powder, and salt.
3. Toss the tofu cubes in the spice mixture until evenly coated.
4. Heat vegetable oil in a skillet over medium-high heat. Fry the tofu in batches for 3-4 minutes per side until golden and crispy.
5. Remove from the skillet and drain on paper towels.
6. Garnish with green onions and serve with rice or vegetables.